STEVEN BERKOFF

The Secret Love Life of Ophelia

faber and faber

First published in 2001
by Faber and Faber Limited
3 Queen Square, London WC1N 3AU

Typeset by Country Setting, Kingsdown, Kent CT14 8ES
Printed in England by Mackays of Chatham plc, Chatham, Kent

A CIP record for this book
is available from the British Library

0-571-20954-8

The Secret Love Life of Ophelia was first performed at the King's Head Theatre, London, on 25 June 2001. The cast was as follows:

HAMLET   Martin Hodgson
OPHELIA   Freya Bosworth

Directed by Steven Berkoff
Music Elliott Davis

THE SECRET LOVE LIFE OF OPHELIA

HAMLET

My dear Ophelia, so many thanks
for entertaining us so charmingly.
'Twas indeed the rarest joy to me
to speak to thee and hear thy graceful skills
manipulate the mysteries of the lute –
and bringing forth such sweet idyllic sounds.
I swear the very birds did cease their chirp
and on their branches listened gratefully.
I pray you will be happy here in Denmark
within the environs of Elsinore,
for though it doth appear at first remote
there is much here I know will interest you.
I will anticipate another visit
where though I sorely lack your sylph-like art
I may perchance beguile you with the flute
or else engage your senses in the wild
to demonstrate our native falconry.
So, my dear new friend, until we meet again,
welcome to Elsinore with all my heart.

Hamlet

OPHELIA

Dear Hamlet and most honoured lord of mine,
thy gracious letter doth too much protest.
My threadbare schoolgirl skills I dared to show,
under command, I strongly haste to add . . .
Since my good father, puffed with paternal pride,
believes his children's offerings precious jewels
and not the simple uncut stones they are,
as doting fathers everywhere I fear,
but your good grace rewards me for my flaws
which makes me doubly in debt to thee.
I'm sure I shall be very happy here
and though I much admired the late King Hamlet
who showered us with such unsought warmth and grace
and see his face so well inscribed in thee
I do not doubt your uncle will restore
the peaceful harmony of Elsinore.
I thank thee for thy generous invitation
and would be humbled to hear thee play thy pipe,
and then to witness those great birds of prey,
which with thy skills thou tam'st so cleverly,
would be an honour more than I deserve . . .

Affectionately,

Ophelia

Ophelia, my new and treasured friend,
O how thy presence doth light up these hours,
when winter drapes our sun in mournful weeds.
You bring to us sweet hints of sparkling spring,
a teasing element of things to come,
just like an early bud sometimes breaks through
the hardened and crisp-frozen wintry soil,
to cheer our hearts and eyes and even souls.
So thou, my dearest friend, art like the bud
that gives us hope and memory of past
when summer clothed our land in joyful bliss,
and so, my dearest flower, I was so fond
to share my simple country sports with thee.
The sun shone hard that day and nature sang
and horses stamped the earth light-heartedly,
as if in thee a kindred soul they found
and your grey dappled beast did seem to fly
like Pegasus, so thrilled to bear thy weight.
Alas I must confess to thee a secret,
that I for once did envy this dumb beast . . .

Hamlet

P.S. Do forgive my last comment if I have overstepped
the bounds of modesty . . .

OPHELIA

Dear lord Hamlet, my most honoured prince,
so many million thanks for such sweet hours,
my spirit soared upon the wind just like
the falcon sweeping so majestically,
and that did faithfully return to thee.
Its powerful wings floated so high and strong
above the strife and turmoil of the world
and though the wind that afternoon was light
its wings did barely tremble on the air,
demanding just the merest kiss of breath
to keep it soaring in empyrean.
So oft I wish I, too, could stride the skies,
and strangely in my dreaming world I do,
as if in some past life I was a bird,
for so familiar is this urge in me,
and when I first awake, 'tween dark and light,
before the veil of night is quite removed,
I sometimes do believe in fact that I . . .
could simply lift my arms, stretch out and fly . . .
What childish wretched thoughts to write to thee!
I blame thy princely generosity
encouraging such words to tumble free.

Ophelia

P.S. You did not step beyond the bounds of modesty.
Your candidness was flattering to me
although I must confess a crimson tide
invaded these pale shores for quite some time . . .

Ophelia, forgive me, oh forgive,
my rude demands upon thy cherished hours,
but dear I must confess to thee the truth,
no sooner hast thou parted from my sight
but I do crave to see thee once again,
as if my thirst is sharpened by what doth quench it,
for thou hast sweetened the dry and austere life,
that I, the sometime heir of this great state,
must take upon my shoulders and the cares
which are the rightful legacy of kings.
This sovereign land I must one day command,
but now, my darling, I cannot command my heart,
since like a stallion stabled up too long,
it pounds against its walls to be set free –
Oh God, I long to feed on pastures green.
So open the stable door and set me free
and ride me hard throughout the glorious day –
beneath the envious Apollo's eye
and spare me not your spurs but gird me on –
guide me, tell me where you wish to go
and I'll obey so readily for thee.

Awaiting your answer impatiently,

Hamlet

P.S. I have a burning secret in my soul
that I, one hour, will sure reveal to thee.

OPHELIA

Dear Hamlet, keep thy secret, keep it deep,
but if it burns then thou must cast it out
and I will cool it for thee with my breath,
until the fiery ember turns to ash,
and then the winds will cast it in the air,
for though thou art the Prince of Denmark
thou hast become king of my heart,
a smaller territory perhaps and yet
its heat doth never vary nor its beat
and now it beats a steadfast drum for thee.
I wish indeed I was a sovereign state –
that thou didst rule with thy benign aspect,
making strict laws that I must sure obey,
and serve thy majesty in mighty wars,
when some audacious nation doth take arms
and saucily makes claim to part of me –
for I, thy land, am yours and yours alone,
the hills and dales, rich forests and flowing brooks,
are all thine own to dally in and play,
and orchards bearing fruit will yield to thee
the heavy sweetness of thy industry –
for know my earth is fertile and so rich,
will give its bounty up to him that toils –
but think it not a toil but some sweet joy
to sweat thy brow in furrowing my fields.
And then demand from me your kingdom's tax
which is to serve and heed your every whim,
for that's the divine right of majesty,
and if I fail to pay my king his due,
then thou must punish me accordingly,
imprisoning me within thy mighty arms;

until my crime, so insolent, is purged,
and if I beg thee for sweet charity,
thou must release me for a little time,
until some new infringement of thy laws
doth summon me to purge my sins again.
And so thy state shall be a happy one,
knowing full well if I obey my king
my life will be abundant and secure,
but if I tarry and withhold the tithe
that every man must render up to thee,
thou wilt be just but most severe with me!

Ophelia

9

Ophelia, oh Ophelia, my love,
how doth thy name drip from my kiss-parched lips
like sweetest honey from a busy hive.
But now dare I to send this letter, thee,
wherein I do confess so shamefully.
I long to pour the passions from my heart,
yet tremble lest I overstep the mark
and wound your ears by being premature
and fear to see thee startle at my words,
as if I was a predatory beast
and thou an innocently grazing hind.
Therefore I will not dare reveal those parts
before my lady gives permission me,
to confess to you how much I yearn for thee.

Hamlet

OPHELIA

Oh, dearest dear, my princely lord,
fear not to trust me with thy burning words,
since I confess I long to send my words to thee,
for lovers whisper secret things when wounded
by the dart of Cupid's trembling bow.
Such honeyed sounds are not for mortal ears,
since those who live in that strange world called love
do speak a different language, that the gods
do take delight in and indeed eavesdrop . . .
and so, my prince, be bold with me and free,
and then I can be brave and bold with thee!

Ophelia

Ophelia, my heart, my girl, is full to overflow.
Like rain-soaked heavy-swollen clouds
that ache to spurt into thy blood-warm earth
nourishing thy seed and bringing forth thy bloom,
my load discharged upon thy perfumed vale
would make me deeper in my love for thee.
Ophelia, I long, I must confess,
to pour the wine of love into thy cup.
My horn doth grow, just like a limb, unwanted
unless it doth conjoin us both in bliss
and so it pines and throbs and yearns for thee.
Thy precious cleft, thy mound, thy blood-red lips
are as a hungry chick within its nest,
its open beak, wide-stretched in nature's need
that my thick worm will satisfy and fill,
crawling through your pulsing heaving soil
and penetrating my Ophelia,
and thrusting, stabbing, twisting, coupling thee.
My blacksmith's bellows melt the stubborn ore,
the magic paste with which God doth create
and now like sap upon the tallest trunk
crawls ever upwards feeding every leaf,
so now my sap is rising to the crest
or like hot molten lava gushing forth
its veins of fire into the trembling earth
my lava seeks to jet from out its rock
and as your flowing river dampens me
I fill thy cup with Hamlet's ecstasy.

Hamlet

My lord and wondrous human lust-filled toy,
thou art a pipe that I would love to play,
making such light delicious-sounding airs
that thou wouldst swoon still deep inside my lair,
but I'd hold back thy seething angry tide
and tease from it some little extra hours,
stroking thy trunk and kissing its silky bark,
wanting its sweetness outliving the long night.
I'd squeeze thy gentle sacks like persimmons,
until thou cried to me, 'Ophelia, mercy . . .'
And then I'd suck thy root so tenderly
until once more the cat desires to spit,
but then I'd bite thy stalk until you howl'd
and so deter thy passion's tidal flow
and as the pain recedes I'd gently claw
the little saddle 'neath your hanging vine
and then thy mighty horn will turn deep red
and as some early dew anoints your tip
I'd scratch thy marble cheeks until they bled!
And so I'd tease and play and make the night
a garden of joy and earthly delights,
rain thy dew inside my love-parched earth
but make each visit last until it hurts.

Ophelia

My dear Ophelia, thou makest me weak,
I read thy words that like a heady wine
fill me with the most dizziest desires.
I dare not even whisper in thine ear
my secret dark and most obsessive love
but through these written words I feel more free
to weave with them my wicked tapestry.
So now the gates are truly down, my love,
my body's thine and now I wish to strap
myself upon thy whitened perfumed deck
like Ulysses, when he, to taste the sound
of sirens on their marshy mist-strewn isle,
did tie himself unto the mast in fear
he would succumb to their most tempting tones,
and then be dashed among the cruel rocks,
but let me, darling, drink thy honeyed songs
and taste the essence of thy secret soul,
let me get drunk upon thy salty seas,
my hot cheeks cooled between thy marble pillars
that would adorn a temple to the gods,
or pour thy sweet libations on my lips
anointing them with creamy healing balm,
my hands gripping each tender moon-like globe
until Diana pleads to let thee go.

Hamlet

Oh generous man, to me thou art too kind,
for while I feel myself imbibed by thee
Be sure, I will not wait to be fulfilled
but clutch thy hard and thick delicious stalk
and like a bon-vivant so gently lick
and dip it slowly, deeply in my mouth
until my gluttony is satisfied
and feel the honey of thy love burst through
and then my raging thirst is slaked by you.
And so I do surrender to thine arms.
What better place on all God's wondrous earth
to thrive than in a lover's warm embrace?
As starlings fly before day shuts her eyes
to nestle in their night-time sanctuaries
and even bats to their own kind do flock,
so loved ones seek each other's souls to cling
and heart to heart and lips to lips do sing
and breath to breath and beating pulse to pulse
until we beat as one, one pounding heart.
Until we wake together like born anew . . .
And know today, sweetheart, my love is you.

Ophelia

My precious and most darling lovely girl,
I will thy sweet voluptuous form enfurl,
enfolding thee just like a chrysalis
and think myself the happiest man on earth.
I ate thy fervent words, my darling one,
as if they were the blessed Eucharist,
the wafer was your downy flesh, your words the wine,
and as it's said our Lord is truly there
within our bodies as we drink his blood,
so you, Ophelia, rest within my breast
whenever I thy fragrant words absorb.
I cannot help when looking in thine eyes
but fall as if into an endless space.
Or when I glance upon thy girlish threads
to feel my very knees unhinge their bolts,
and watch your ivory hands flutter through space,
I think of butterflies and precious doves
and deeply wish they would alight on me.
And then I catch the faintest, lightest scent,
your hair's soft odour, deeply breathe it in
as if it were the elixir of life,
and when I hear your voice from distant rooms
all other sounds of life straight away go dumb
and yours the only melody I can hear,
and when you walk away from me, my babe,
my eyes do cling to your receding form
and do believe a miracle was born;
each perfect limb and joint in harmony,
but sad I am to see the gulf grow wide

and pray you'll turn a little, just a curve,
to bring your sweetness back again to me.

Hamlet

OPHELIA

Oh, my mignon, thy words do feast on me
each one is like a tiny mouth that draws
my salty tears or else sweet tears of lust,
thy words are like a web that round me weaves
and I, thy willing victim, wrapped inside
and thou, my spider, come when hunger calls
and feed upon my life, my heart and soul . . .
O feast upon me, sir, and drain me dry,
leave nothing left of me so I might live
within you day and night and never part.
I loathe this world that separates us both,
making our pain the blessèd songs we sing
to lullaby ourselves into a sleep.
If only thou wert not a royal prince
that must for thy great nation be a lamb
to sacrifice to make thy country strong,
by spreading thy seed into some unloved hag
who has a royal pedigree to sell.
A farmer's wife, I envy so much more
whose man just vents his lust upon a whim,
her skirts flown high as in the yellow fields
so rampantly they drink each other's fill
as if by right they state their lusty claims,
yet you with all your princely attributes
your brilliant luminosity and gifts
and all the power that in your future lies
cannot anoint me with a stolen kiss!

Ophelia

Ophelia, Ophelia my soul,
I want no palaces or stately homes
no ceremony with stitched and empty smiles
no wedding made that's not in heaven blessed
no body next to mine devoid of love
no wretched violation of my sex
no life of sour regrets and painful thoughts
no if I only did this, if I did that
no waking to a stranger in my bed
no life without my darling loving sweet.
No to what is politically expedient
no to whores and harlots for the state
no to those whose blood is cold and dead,
but to live each day and know that I'll see thee
to awake as if in waking I still dream
to disbelieve that now the daylight breaks
to discover thy hair on a pillowcase
to sense thy silken breath upon my cheek
to feel my darling's thigh rest on my leg
to know that thou art deep in gentle dream
to see a little smile play on thy lips
to thank the angels for this unique gift
to wake thee gently with a dewy kiss . . .

I will, believe me, oh my dearest heart,
give thee a million stolen kisses more
and with the interest I would triple them
far more than any usurious grasping Jew.
I'd scale the ramparts hoist up by desire,
I'd find thee in the secretest place on earth,
I'd batter down the portals with my ram

and rain thee down in kisses hot and thick
until thou begged and gasped for breath to live
so thou couldst suck down many thousand kisses
    more . . .
And then once more thou'dst beg for precious air
but then I'd make thee suck the air from me
so that thy lips and mine were ever entwined
and I the planet where thu fedst and drank
so that thou'dst never need, nor miss, nor pine.

Hamlet

OPHELIA

Dear darling Hamlet, insubstantial love,
my noble prince but more my heart and soul
and even more than that my tongue and lips
that have no purpose than to taste thy kiss,
so food and drink abominate my mouth
that hungers for the stronger taste of thee,
and if for food I'd feed upon thy lips
I'd never feel the pangs of want or thirst,
since thy abundant kisses fill me deep,
so graciously I'll accept all thy debts
and interest that has therefore since accrued,
but more than words the contract must be filled.
I need the hand that wrote the sacred text
to write his burning words now on my flesh,
I cannot hold my trembling quill which shakes,
carrying such responsibility,
those treasured words of my fidelity.
The very ink I use turns into blood
since every stroke draws from my swollen heart
the life I wish to pass only with thee.
So write upon me all those singeing words
thou hast so many minutes, hours, days,
caressed the white insensate parchment sheets,
oh, how I envy them thy constant stroke.
Now trace upon my burning yielding flesh
those symbols of thy promises, my lord.
I have thy bond and now demand the gold,
I needs must feel thy words turned into acts,
now take thy opportunity, be bold!

Ophelia

HAMLET

What acts, my darling, tell me what thou thinkst?
Although it's true, I know it all too well,
but hunger for confession from thy lips,
since thy bold words doth make my body swell
as if the words themselves were fingers, hands
and kisses too on my soft flesh that grows,
I blush to tell thee, on the thoughts of thee,
just as a modest rose doth proudly swell
when summer's golden streams doth stroke its cheeks,
but I must part from thee in haste, alas,
since Rosencrantz and Guildenstern arrive
to pay their salutations to the King
and as for him, one day I will disgorge
the secret that is buried in my breast;
but now I must needs entertain these pests
yet absence from thee keeps my flame alive.

Hamlet

OPHELIA

Dearest darling devoted and damnèd love,
what acts thou asks and yet confess thou know'st?
Yet *I'll* confess and barely can describe
since blood invades my cheeks like Cupid slapped
me for my brazen and audacious sighs.
Thy words, thou know'st the very words thou wrote,
need I remind my bawdy lord of these,
when thou didst dip thy quill into thy pot
didst thou not say . . . 'I wish this quill was me
and thee the pot,' the nectar in which thou sought.
But know, dear heart, my pot doth overflow
and waits too long for thy bold pen to dip.
Alone in my maid's bed, my naked flesh
awaits thy fervent strokes with eagerness.
But now my lips will read your honeyed words
circle my heaving breast with paragraphs
making my nipples rising crests, full stops,
to stop thy mouth until they're swallowed up,
then let thy sentences begin their trek,
climbing the curving valleys of the moon,
descending oh so slowly till they reach
the forest where thy verse may take a breath,
but now the words explore a new terrain,
full overgrown with branches, there to shade
thy saucy metaphors from sun's strong glare . . .
But now thy verbs have found a secret stream
within a ravine where they wish to slake
their burning thirst and drink like lusty beasts,
and now the words come bolder as if they're drunk,
for this, a magic trough is ne'er drained dry

the more thy tongues do lap the more it fills.
They now become pioneers and stake their claims,
on every hill and dale and brook and cave.

Ophelia

Dear one, my treasure, my own beloved girl,
your letter was a healing balm to me
to rub into my wounds, my love-pierced heart,
shot by the arrows of outrageous fortune
that keeps our love infamously apart.
I drank your words down like a man possessed;
my veins did burn with such a divine fire
that suddenly I saw thy blessed face
and dreamed, we lay together side by side,
but as you lay, Diana-like so pure,
I held my breath, I dared not even speak
lest this most glorious dream, this phantasm,
should melt, dissolve as dreams are wont to do,
just at that very moment that you consummate,
just at the point of divine bliss, the best
of womanhood in your arms and ready yes
to taste this ecstasy, this heady wine-rich kiss,
then all at once . . . you're grasping empty space!
A pillowcase that once was her soft face,
the ruffled sheets once acted out her limbs.
But no, not last night, something heaven sent,
for you did not torment me within my bed,
to cruelly disappear just like a jest,
since gods do love to tease our happiness . . .
You stayed, my darling, stayed and something more,
it felt . . . as if we melted into one.
I seemed to feel your heart within my breast,
your hands were gripping mine and fingers twined,
oh darling, strange it was, delirious,
my lips were yours, my thighs felt like your thighs,
I felt my hand or your hand guiding mine,

as your most delicate fingers did explore
the burning centre of my universe.
Slowly, slowly moving like a cat
towards its languid and unsuspecting prey,
but this prey was not sleepy but alert,
just bursting, swollen, bloated, gorged with blood,
as painfully you moved each finger forth,
a hairsbreadth at a time, oh painful bliss,
I could not bear, I swear, much more of this,
my tendons stretching, teeth biting my lips,
the merest whisper further, fingertips
now just a crack away, oh stop my mouth
and thrust in there your weaving pretty tongue
so I might, no, oh please not, quite despair.
Heaven's burning, my hand did cup your head,
as I sucked up kisses from the ocean bed,
still fearful – will this magic dream dissolve?
When now, just then, your hand did slowly draw
my quiver, slowly felt it grasp and thread
your bow and then the stars, they seemed to burst
and then from them I made a string of pearls
that thou mightst wear upon thy ivory breast.

Hamlet

Thank you darling for the sweetest pearls
that ever woman could so proudly wear.
They glisten on my skin like tiny moons
and sometimes when I put the moon to bed
I swallow them, just like the day engulfs
Diana's mighty sphere and wait impatiently
for night to come and pray you'll make more pearls.
But now the watchdogs are abroad, my love,
I fervently implore you to make haste
and deliver those sacred moons to me yourself.
I am just so amused when brother Laertes
warns me of 'the canker' and 'the bud'
with face so serious whilst I must act the maid
and little knows, poor innocent, that the bud
has flowered full and one black bumblebee
has sucked the honey, oh, so many times
whilst happily my petals have engulfed
the creature snuggling in my garden womb.

Ophelia

Dear heart,
I will so desperately upon this night
attempt to put my words into hot deeds;
and so, Ophelia, await my knock,
upon the stroke of twelve I will be there.
Oh darling I am trembling with the thought,
and fear you are an insubstantial dream,
and I shall wake into a bitter world
with no Ophelia to make it sweet,
but only coldly grim and censoring brothers,
o'erweening and joy-stealing fathers
and most lewd and unrespecting mothers,
and lastly, the most vile and loathsome uncles,
and yet all these, these truly cankered blooms,
appoint themselves the gardeners of our souls,
as if these weeds which drain the nourishing soil
were now rare orchids and the pungent rose.

And so mankind stewed in corruption's ways
doth overturn the order of the world
where nature seeks its right ascendancy,
where lovers mate through true affinity
through passion's mutual desire and love
that grows like nature in which we are a part,
the sun is God's abundant flowing love
for all the living moving things of earth . . .
it doth not shine on privilege and the rich
leaving small scraps for those in humble homes.
If this were so the world would soon decay
and rot and evil things that darkly thrive
would dominate this wild majestic orb.

Nor are we dogs that must be smartly bred
to keep the line intact until it's weak,
and can claim nothing virile, bold or strong,
except the name to which it dearly hopes
the vigorous and healthy will bow low –
but we are spirits of another sort
and as you know true love's first made in heaven
and no force on earth can sunder it,
and so until midnight I shall be mute.

I watch the clock until those hands point north.
To lovers' eyes they scarcely seem to budge
while to the condemned man time seems to fly,
and so I shall pretend that I am he
awaiting to be hanged upon midnight
but oh, this hanging wait I eagerly!

Hamlet

OPHELIA

Oh sweetest and most darling love of mine,
while I was floating between heaven and earth
anticipating every single joy –
since you are joy personified to me –
I fed upon the nectar of your words
lest I should die of thirst 'fore midnight come,
and so I plucked from out my secret store
those precious letters that contain your heart.
Oh how my blood did heat again in lust
warmed by the burning embers of your words,
when, just then, with eyes half-closed to blur
the world outside so I might be alone
with thee and make the waiting minutes lighter,
rude horrid sounds tore through the love-smote air,
and ripped it all to a thousand thousand shreds.
My father crying, 'What is *that* you read?'
and snatched the emblem of your noble love
from my struck numb and most fear-frozen hands.
Before I could protest to him, 'My love
for him is sacred and by angels blessed,'
he mocked the words with shouts and villainous threats.
'Don't even dare to touch it with your hands,'
I howled, 'lest you defile its purity.'
For that, he says, he will expose us to the King.
So, my brave and most adored by me,
tonight, this special night now cannot be,
but think of me all through the darkened hours
and I like Eurydice will think of thee;
so, be an Orpheus and sing to me

and send your thoughts across the starlit skies.
I'll stay awake and listen, but now be wise.

Ophelia

Ophelia, my dearest darling heart,
I share your torments, each and every one,
what pains you finds its echo swift in me,
as sunlight warms the rich and poor alike
so every woe that strikes you is a blow
that doubly falls upon my weary head.
And so with raging heart I will be brief . . .
Poor thing, you let the bird out of the cage . . .
But let it fly, it will grow stronger wings
for being out at last and unconfined.
For now they can do nothing, not unless
they exile you and try to sever us.
Oh fiery hell and damnèd spite to think
this old and crusty slave will soil our love,
and like those mean and bitter foes of Cupid,
those on whom he never wastes his darts
now do hate the love they cannot make.
Oh how they loathe the raging lovers' fires,
that they can never, never will inspire!

Hamlet

Dear, special and most beautiful of men,
your words inspire me always to be brave
for I was weak as if struck through my heart,
but thy good words I used to stitch my wounds
and now it beats more strongly than before.
And now, my own dear life, I have a plan,
since we must now alleviate their fears,
small-minded people must be pacified,
so we might just continue as before,
the more we shout our loves up to the sky
the more walls they will build to hinder it,
the more portcullises and dreadful moats,
so darling please observe my modest scheme.
They fear the love that cannot be controlled
for they cannot exploit it to their ends;
then let us now pretend our love is soured,
that this exposure has besmirched your pride,
exposing your true soul for all to mock,
and now thou hatest my careless wantonness.
My father wants to shame us to the King
and set me loose upon your nightly strolls
so that the hidden Claudius may observe
as I return your letters and precious gifts.
So Hamlet show no vestiges of love,
be an *angry* prince and boldly scold,
I was a whim, thou'lt say, a passing fling,
A rash indulgence of youth's heated blood
before stern wisdom trims the burning flame.
I know you'll say you'd rather cut your tongue
than soil that special instrument that God
did give us to express our truth, but think

you are an actor playing out a role,
act harshly then and flay me with your tongue
while secretly your inner soul doth wink!

Ophelia

34

O my most precious unalloyed pure joy,
O how it pained me more than thou canst guess
to hurl at thee those wicked deprecations
but to speak true the more I deeply loved
the harsher and more villainous was my tongue,
so thou shouldst know the very worst my bark,
the greater my devotion to my love,
so in this way I still made love to thee.
And using thus this code you must translate,
reversing every sentence that I said
and gathering momentum like an actor
who once inflamed upon his role becomes
the very fiction he impersonates.
So when I cried out loud 'I loved thee not'
the more it meant I loved thee more than life,
since starved of life which is the very breath
we die and likewise missing you I die;
but then I saw thee wince and some small tears
did form, I prayed to God they were not real
but actor's artifice in heat of play,
but then I almost lost my character
and wished to hold you in my arms and heal.

Hamlet

OPHELIA

Sweetest and most divine angel of mine,
my tears were real, so salty real they gushed
from out a soul brim full of perfect joy,
for know, I spied the brilliance of thine art,
the worst, the bitterest fruit you made me eat,
was turned to sweetest honey in my heart.
The words you used to flay my hungry soul
were as the softest silk caressing me,
the loud stern sounds that bruised the very air
became sweet music to me in my ears . . .
So no, dear soul, I did obey the rules,
and they the audience who came to hear
a tragedy of broken love, despised,
will go back to their homes well satisfied,
while we, the actors celebrate our play
and live, my love, to play another day!

Ophelia

HAMLET

Oh my most fair and brilliant girl,
such arts you have to fool the idiot world,
which needs the outer form of all things true,
the gesture, grin and wink they swallow up
unable to observe the inner life,
the pulse, the beat, the sap that flows.
Instead they think cheap gilt is precious gold,
a compliment from oily sycophants,
a true assessment of their dirty souls.
They think that vulgar wealth bespeaks respect,
not avaricious greed and often theft.
And love is just a grubby word they use
to grace a letter's end of lying prose;
my God, you'd get more value from the Jews.
They think great art's the latest monkey's scrawl,
they're so afraid to say just what they mean
in case the trash some idiot defecates
is then revealed to have some obscure sheen.
As for the play, their low abysmal wit
applauds as genius some puerile shit
since they can see their ugly face in it.
So if they fail to see our burning love,
if they fail to see beneath the game,
if they fail to understand that God demands
a fusion of two souls when nature mates,
they fail God's purpose for the human race.
The sun conceives with earth and fertile sea
to create her wild majestic progeny,
the moon mates with the yearning tides,
the rain brings forth tumultuous flowers,
the bee, the ox, the cat, the awesome bear

do all conjoin with wind and sun and air
to populate this pretty world with life,
so why, oh why, on our God's valued earth
should we be any different to all forms
that want, nay more, that passionately do need
the spark of mutual desire and love?

Hamlet

OPHELIA

O my love, my life, my own dear heart,
your words enwrap me and do comfort me
as if they were your own strong arms and hands
whose absence from my flesh wraps me in grief,
such grief that each new day is not a birth
to celebrate but just a little death,
since life sans you is a small death to me,
for death dissolves all bonds, all unities.
The most devoted passionate and hot love
cannot compete with death's more icy fangs . . .
So when the grinning sceptre scythes our lives
as he must do to all of us poor souls
we must then say our lives have been a gift,
and each new day, nay each new heartbeat, breath,
a tiny miracle bestowed on all of us,
and what a sin, a mortal sin to waste
the living tissue that we occupy
by not fulfilling life, not giving thanks,
not celebrating this most intimate gift,
instead to waste, to mourn each passing day.
Now would a gardener so neglect his field,
to let the valued fruit rot on the branch,
allow the noxious weed to crawl and thrive
and suffocate the bloom and sap the life?
And are we not more valuable than a field,
and are our lives not gardens that we must tend
and nurse with such a reverent care,
and are we not this precious yielding earth
so capable of giving birth to forms

most wondrous and, with you, most beautiful?
I am your earth, oh prince, neglect me not!

Ophelia

HAMLET

My love, my love and my own darling child,
how clearly you define our sorry waste,
the loss of minutes, hours, days and years,
that causes me to question life itself
and whether 'tis nobler in the mind to suffer
or take arms against this sea of troubles . . .
The former rises in my soul just like
a ship poised on a precipitous wave
unknowing if it be dashed rudely down
into the ocean's dark infernal grave
or else with wit and navigator's skills
we plough those mountainous sky-scraping hills.
Oh how my thoughts like poor tormented ghosts
do batter at my skull to be set free
or else like savage winds they turn my sails
when I would into thy sweet harbour seek
the sanctuary and warm comfort of thy arms,
the safest place and free from any harm.

Hamlet

OPHELIA

My sweetest, sweetest, sweetest darling lord,
thou must reveal thy secret, give it me,
since it doth weigh thee down like heavy chains
upon some poor convicted miscreant,
let me be trusted to release thy bonds.
Do not despair, my lover, for I sink
with thee since I am tied to thee with knots
of love that's stronger than the hardest steel,
and when you falter then I too will fall,
and when you rise, my spirit rises too,
exhilaration puffed and oh so light,
ready to ascend beyond the mountains' height
and onto the moon, the stars and far beyond . . .
but now I am on earth and missing thee,
please come and tend my gardens, please my lord,
and pull those ugly weeds disturbing me.

Ophelia

O Ophelia, my dearest and sweet love,
thou art the fertile earth that I must till,
husband the shoots that presently will burst
from out the yielding and warm-natured soil.
Yes, thou art a garden that I must tend
for I, too, fear the rank and poisonous weeds,
that seek to suck thy youth and strangle thee.
But trust me, my own and rare sweet flower,
that I will cut them down and root them out!
No noxious and repellent slugs will thrive,
no nettles hiding in thy friendly grass,
no snakes entwined within thy branches' shade
to bite with loathsome and obnoxious bile.
There is a serpent, darling, within our glade,
our little orchard where we often roamed
as children when amazed at butterflies
and all the wonders of the magic world,
this snake waits hidden with its twitching tongue
to once more sink his greedy loathsome fangs
into our innocent and unsuspecting flesh,
but this time I will be ready, never fear,
to cut the monster's evil head right off.
There is a play tonight before the thing
I talk about, our wise and self-made King.
Please come, for darling, all will soon be clear,
the secret soon will out for all to hear,
of course, like strolling players we must conceal
our throbbing hearts beneath the smiling mask
so no one will suspect our secret jest.

Till later, oh my darling heart, I ache
to hold my precious softest turtle dove.

Hamlet

Dear prince and lord of all that I possess,
it was astonishing I must confess
and thought my pounding heart would burst,
not knowing what thou hadst contrived for us
and then thou nearly gav'st the game away,
you wicked boy, to say, 'How fair a thought
to lie between maids' legs', I blushed to death.
And then thy play did mightily disturb
the King, who rose as if thy words did bite,
or lance some sore that he was keen to hide,
for never did I see him so alarmed,
his blood did from his face seem to withdraw,
as if in shame to serve those eyes and ears
that heard something that deeply pained his soul,
or witnessed something they could not endure.
His pallor then did turn sickly and white,
but now in brief I heard a plan tonight,
too terrible for my ears to comprehend,
for they, my father and the King, do scheme
to exile thee, my love, to foreign shores . . .
Oh horrible, horrible and most horrible,
and so thy mother plans to question thee
as if in confidence to probe thy soul
to give thee one more chance to prove thyself,
but other prying ears will scoop thy drift . . .
My father, wicked man, and not content
to murder our most natural new-born love,

now seeks the clues that he doth plan to use
to seal thy fate, be warned my love, in haste!

Always,

Ophelia

P.S. Be calm and feed them lying anecdotes
or they will raise the drawbridge to our hearts.

Dear love, the bloody deed, I fear, is done.
Poor soul, thy father, but interfering man –
did feel at last my venom's piercing stick –
discovered all too late how dangerous
it is to rob the savage eagle's nest,
for she will claw your eyes out of your head,
nor will a lioness not tear your flesh
from off your bones if you do threat its cub.
So all the more I needs protect our love
from those malicious predators that stalk
and prey like filthy vultures on the young.
So must all love, for love creates the world –
and those that interfere must pay the price
as if they were conspiring to destroy
the future of our blessed human race.
Forgive me if I could not heed thy words
or simulate a calm I do not have
nor act the loving and the contrite son –
whilst knowing that a dirty spider lurked
feeding on our lives, our words, our souls,
and then regurgitating it to him,
the most dangerous spider of them all . . .
I beg thee to forgive me, dear Ophelia,
for I was lost in rage and sick with gall,
as if we were just toys to take apart,
to satisfy some lazy infant's whim,
I could not help but strike back at the cause.
But I do miss thee sorely, dear Ophelia,
and will upon the stroke of twelve this night
rap very softly on thy bedroom door –
the guardian of it now, thank God, is gone –

but *I* will be thy father and thy love,
protecting thee from every pain and woe,
and this I promise to eternity.
The King dare not as yet imprison me
for he doth know Polonius's lonely death
was the just fruit of his own treachery.
Now Claudius makes his plans in swiftest haste,
to have me stowed aboard at first daybreak,
oh darling, how I dearly long for thee!

Hamlet

OPHELIA

O Hamlet, I am so very sick at heart,
oh why couldst thou not frame thy tongue?
Although God sees only too well I'm sure
and straightway will forgive thy murderous act.
But I, my dazzling and my only love
cannot help but mourn for his cruel death.
He was the father of my blood and life,
and although intolerant of our special love,
he was an agent to his master's voice.
I fear I did provoke thee to this act,
and now I writhe in torment's hellish fires –
I have lost everything, both him and thee,
for thee, my comfort and my only hope,
my sanctuary and my source of joy,
must now be taken far away from me –
my soul will pine but I shall wait for thee,
for though thou tookst a maid and made her yours
be sure I'll love thee Hamlet evermore,
and evermore and evermore and ever . . .

Ophelia

Oh my prophetic soul, with that one deed,
I pierced the daughter through the father's greed,
and then I wounded thee and I am slain,
Ophelia, my darling love, I die
without the vital food that nourishes me.
Don't let me go without one glimpse of thee
without one lingering kiss, that it may feed
my starving heart till once again we meet –

Hamlet

I crave you, need you more than you could know –
but alas I sink into the raging pits
where my grave sins do leer and spit at me
and feel the fires of hell lick at my feet,
so I must penance pay until those wrongs
are purged, and pray my sins are washed away.
So Jesus asks that I make sacrifice –
what greater sacrifice can then I make
than denying to my love-starved eyes
my own dear darling's so familiar face
that I do dream about by day and night,
do stroke it and caress thy lips and cheeks.
I love the way thy eyebrow shapes those orbs
that I could stare at, long, long minutes, hours,
until thou weariedst, to be so adored –
and love thy chestnut hair that tumbled free
for me to comb with fingers eagerly,
and kiss the nape, my favourite special part,
and for dessert I'd nibble thy earlobe,
that tiny silken pendant, a hanging peach,
but since I'm now so very close to thee
I have to trace your jaw-line with my breath
until I reach that little pouty curve,
those sweet-ripe cherries that I long to bite,
thy lips which are so dangerous to me.
And now so near I have to visit thee
and knock upon the door with my hot tongue,
oh let me in, it says, I wish to play,
the portcullis did open and in I leapt.
Poor you I could not leave you till I supped
full deep upon that potent heady wine,

but now I must your precious words conceal
within my deepest and most secret part –
where no one but myself will ever claim
or stain with eyes and fingers or will mock
the letters they were never meant to read –
so my lord of life and my best love,
the end of words, the holy book is closed –
I love thee till it hurts too much to speak,
I love thee as if my life was born for this –
I'll love thee until the very end of time
or when they say our saviour comes again
and graves will open up and dead will rise,
and even then I'll wait for my bold sire,
and if we cannot speak again, just if,
I'll know on earth I tasted sweetest bliss.

Ophelia

Dear love, is this the last I'll hear of thee?
As I reluctantly depart these shores,
I give these humble words to our dear boy,
the messenger who like a Mercury
doth fly 'twixt you and me with lightning speed,
and there he stands and patiently doth wait,
as I do sadly write these final words.
He glances down at me as if he reads
our letters with his heart for there they lay
since there he plants them safe within his vest
protecting them as if they were his babes.
So now, and just for now, farewell my love,
for I do love thee now and evermore.
'Tis said in ancient time that man and woman
were united as one being sharing
heart and soul and blood in harmony,
and that some ancient god did sunder us
in anger for some sin and since that day,
we have been crawling through the endless earth
searching most desperately for our lost half –
and pining in our lonely misery.
For such a task is like the curse of Sisyphus,
condemned for ever to heave his mighty rock
which only tumbles down to where it was –
so having found my perfect other half
I cannot bear to let thee go again –
with thee I felt my heart and body sing
with joy so rapturous, I'm sure God smiled
to see two lost souls once again unite.
And now I go, I am so sick at heart,
I kiss you tenderly and hold your head

between my hands and pray it won't be long
that we are far apart, I will come back –
since you possess, my love, half of my heart.

Hamlet

On eagle's wings carry my frenzied words,
deliver them to him my eternal love,
then wait for him to give thee back *his* words.
Oh I am so very weak at heart –
the days are like lost worlds in which I breathe
to no avail and have no taste to eat,
but seek only forgetfulness and peace –
and morning's light is just a bitter curse
and then I pray for darkness and deep dreams
and in that hopeful world you will appear
and keep me company, oh valiant wish.
And when my darling does appear I hate
the morning light that melts my love away,
and wish the precious living hours gone
since they are dead in absence of the love
which keeps my purpose in this world alive.
But now I fear my candle's growing dim,
it wanes for want of thy sweet living breath.
O Hamlet, I am not afraid to die,
'For in that sleep of death what dreams may come?'
Remember when you spoke those words to me,
and since you visit me only in dreams
it may be there that we shall meet again –

Ophelia

HAMLET

Ophelia, my dearest and most adored love,
it took so long before your bitter words
did cross the angry and resentful sea
as if the waves themselves could not endure
the sorrow that they had to bear.
Through many faithful hands your letter passed,
each one protecting it, as if it was
your very own and precious beating heart –
that thou didst send to me to save my life
for my own heart was cold and hard and dead,
not beating fast in lovers' sweet embrace,
and so what need my heart to do its work,
for what except to see thee dear again?
Oh let God's mighty drummer cease his beat
for why should he thus toil his life in vain? –
but then I too did dream, sweet love, of thee
and cradled thee so gently in my arms,
for lovers meet in dreams though far apart
and by such means they really know they love
for true love's thoughts ascend into the air
just like the dainty wings of butterflies
and so our spirits did make love in dreams,
that rare and special world where only those
not weighted down with evil thoughts may enter.
But now we'll make our dreams real flesh and blood,
for now I am returning back to thee.
I know what I must do, my thoughts are clear,
and thou shalt know it all when face to face,
and every minute thou hast been in pain
an hour of blessed heaven shall be thine,
for every bitter tear that thou hast shed

I'll plant for thee the sweetest smelling rose,
for every wound a thousand soft caresses
and every lonely second thou hast passed
an inventory shall be swiftly made
and thy investment of such painful woe
with kisses shall be repaid a thousand fold.
Ophelia, my darling, be at peace,
for I do send my beating heart to thee!

Hamlet

*Ophelia's spot is now absent and we hear Gertrude
saying the words of Ophelia's drowning . . .*

GERTRUDE

'There is a willow grows aslant the brook
That shows his hoar leaves in the glassy stream:
Therewith fantastic garlands did she make
Of crowflowers, nettles, daisies and long purples,
That liberal shepherds give a grosser name,
But our cold maids do dead men's fingers call them.
There on the pendent boughs her coronet weeds
Clambering to hang, an envious sliver broke,
When down her weedy trophies and herself
Fell in the weeping brook. Her clothes spread wide,
And mermaidlike awhile they bore her up
Which time she chanted snatches of old lauds,
As one incapable of her own distress,
Or like a creature native and endued
Unto that element. But long it could not be
Till that her garments, heavy with their drink
Pulled the poor wretch from her melodious lay
To muddy death . . . '

Hamlet is speechless.
Slow fade on his tormented face.

The Secret Love Life of Ophelia

Steven Berkoff is an actor, director and playwright.
Some of his plays are *East*, *West*, *Sink the Belgrano!*,
Decadence, *Kvetch* and *Acapulco*. His theatre books
include *I am Hamlet*, *Overview*, *Meditations on
Metamorphosis*, the photographic book *The Theatre
of Steven Berkoff* and his autobiography *Free
Association*. Among his film credits are *A Clockwork
Orange*, *Octopussy*, *Beverly Hills Cop* and his own
production of *Decadence*. He lives in London.

by the same author

PLAYS ONE
(*East, West, Greek, Sink the Belgrano!, Massage, Lunch,
The Bow of Ulysses, Sturm und Drang*)

PLAYS TWO
(*Decadence, Kvetch, Acapulco, Harry's Christmas,
Brighton Beach Scumbags, Dahling You Were Marvellous,
Dog, Actor*)

PLAYS THREE
(*Ritual in Blood, The Messiah, Oedipus*)

FREE ASSOCIATION: AN AUTOBIOGRAPHY

Ray Bradbury, one of the greatest writers of SF, fantasy and horror fiction in the world today, has published some 500 short stories, novels, plays and poems since his first story appeared in *Weird Tales* when he was twenty years old. Among his many famous works are *Fahrenheit 451*, *The Illustrated Man* and *The Martian Chronicles*. He has also written the screenplays for *It Came from Outer Space*, *Something Wicked This Way Comes* and *Moby Dick*. Mr Bradbury was Idea Consultant for the United States Pavilion at the 1964 World's Fair, has written the basic scenario for the interior of Spaceship Earth at EPCOT, Disney World, and is doing consultant work on city engineering and rapid transit. When one of the Apollo Astronaut teams landed on the moon, they named Dandelion Crater there to honour Mr Bradbury's novel, *Dandelion Wine*. Mr Bradbury recently flew in an aeroplane for the first time.

Mr Bradbury is currently collaborating with Jimmy Webb on lyrics for a musical version of his *Dandelion Wine*. His opera, *Fahrenheit 451*, opened in the autumn of 1988. He has been asked to help design a twenty-first-century city to be built near Tokyo and has recently completed a new novel.

By the same author

The Martian Chronicles (The Silver Locusts)
The Golden Apples of the Sun
Moby Dick (screenplay)
Dandelion Wine
The October Country
The Illustrated Man
The Small Assassin
The Day it Rained Forever
Something Wicked This Way Comes
I Sing the Body Electric!
The Halloween Tree
The Machineries of Joy
The Wonderful Ice Cream Suit
When Elephants Last in the Dooryard Bloomed
R is for Rocket
S is for Space
Long After Midnight
The Stories of Ray Bradbury (vols 1 & 2)
*Where Robot Mice and Robot Men Run Round in Robot
 Towns*
Death Is A Lonely Business
The Toynbee Convector